being God's man...
by understanding a woman's heart

Real Men. Real Life. Powerful Truth.

Stephen Arterburn
Kenny Luck & Todd Wendorff

WATERBROOK
PRESS

contents

Welcome to the Every Man Bible Study Series v

How to Use This Study Guide vii

Introduction: *Can You Relate?* 1

Session 1   Trust! 5
              I Want the Right Motive

Session 2   Acceptance 14
              I Want to Be Loved with Christlike Love

Session 3   Connection 21
              I Want You to Know Me Before You "Know" Me

Session 4   Headship 30
              I Want Spiritual Leadership

Session 5   Encouragement 38
              I Want to Feel Special to You

Session 6   Friendship 47
              I Want "Us"

Session 7   Thoughtfulness 55
              I Want to Be Remembered by You

Session 8   Compassion 63
              I Want a Strong Man with a Soft Heart

SMALL-GROUP RESOURCES

Leader Tips 73

Using This Study in a Large-Group Format 78

Prayer Request Record 80
Defining Group Roles 81
Small-Group Roster 82
Spiritual Checkup 83
Small-Group Covenant 86

welcome to the every man
Bible study series

As Christian men, we crave true-to-life, honest, and revealing Bible study curricula that will equip us for the battles that rage in our lives. We are looking for resources that will get us into our Bibles in the context of mutually accountable relationships with other men. But like superheroes who wear masks and work hard to conceal their true identities, most of us find ourselves isolated and working alone on the major issues we face. Many of us present a carefully designed public self while hiding our private self from view. This is not God's plan for us.

Let's face it. We all have trouble being honest with ourselves, particularly in front of other men.

As developers of a men's ministry, we believe that many of the problems among Christian men today are direct consequences of an inability to practice biblical openness—being honest about our struggles, questions, and temptations—and to connect with one another. Our external lives may be in order, but storms of unprocessed conflict, loss, and fear are eroding our resolve to maintain integrity. Sadly, hurting Christian men are flocking to unhealthy avenues of relief instead of turning to God's Word and to one another.

We believe the solution to this problem lies in creating opportunities for meaningful relationships among men. That's why we designed this Bible study series to be thoroughly interactive. When a man practices biblical openness with other men, he moves from secrecy to candor, from isolation to connection, and from pretense to authenticity.

Kenny and Todd developed the study sessions at Saddleback Church in Lake Forest, California, and at King's Harbor Church in Redondo Beach, California, where they teach men's Bible studies. At these studies men hear an outline of the Bible passage, read the verses together, and then answer a group discussion question at their small-group tables. The teaching pastor then facilitates further discussion within the larger group.

This approach is a huge success for many reasons, but the key is that, deep down, men really do want close friendships with other guys. We don't enjoy living on the barren islands of our own secret struggles. However, many men choose to process life, relationships, and pressures individually because they fear the vulnerability required in small-group gatherings. *Suppose someone sees behind my carefully constructed image? Suppose I encounter rejection after revealing one of my worst sins?* Men willingly take risks in business and the stock market, sports and recreation, but we do not easily risk our inner lives.

Many church ministries are now helping men win this battle, providing them with opportunities to experience Christian male companionship centered in God's Word. This study series aims to supplement and expand that good work around the country. If these lessons successfully reach you, then they will also reach every relationship and domain that you influence. That is our heartfelt prayer for every man in your group.

how to use this study guide

As you prepare for each session, first review the **Key Verse** and **Goals for Growth,** which reveal the focus of the study at hand. Discuss as a group whether or not you will commit to memorizing the Key Verse for each session. The **Head Start** section then explains why these goals are necessary and worthwhile. Each member of your small group should complete the **Connect with the Word** section *before* the small-group sessions. Consider this section to be your personal Bible study for the week. This will ensure that everyone has spent some time interacting with the biblical texts for that session and is prepared to share responses and personal applications. (You may want to mark or highlight any questions that were difficult or particularly meaningful so you can focus on those during the group discussion.)

When you gather in your small group, you'll begin by reading aloud the **Head Start** section to remind everyone of the focus for the current session. The leader will then invite the group to share any questions, concerns, insights, or comments arising from their personal Bible study during the past week. If your group is large, consider breaking into subgroups of three or four people (no more than six) at this time.

Next, get into **Connect with the Group,** starting with the **Group Opener.** These openers are designed to get at the heart of each week's lesson. They focus on how the men in your group relate to the passage and topic you are about to discuss. The group leader will read aloud the opener for that week's session and then facilitate interaction on the **Discussion Questions** that follow. (Remember: Not everyone has to offer an answer for every question.)

Leave time after your discussion to complete the **Standing Strong** exercises, which challenge each man to consider, *What's my next move?* As you openly express your thoughts to the group, you'll be able to hold one another accountable to reach for your goals.

Finally, close in **prayer,** either in your subgroups or in the larger group. You may want to use this time to reflect on and respond to what God has done in your group during the session. Also invite group members to share their personal joys and concerns, and use this as "grist" for your prayer time together.

By way of review, each lesson is divided into the following sections:

To be read or completed *before* the small-group session:
• **Key Verse**
• **Goals for Growth**
• **Head Start**
• **Connect with the Word** (home Bible study: 30-40 minutes)

To be completed *during* the small-group session:
• Read aloud the **Head Start** section (5 minutes)
• Discuss personal reaction to **Connect with the Word** (10 minutes)
• **Connect with the Group** (includes the **Group Opener** and discussion of the heart of the lesson: 30-40 minutes)
• **Standing Strong** (includes having one person pray for the group; challenges each man to take action: 20 minutes)

can you relate?

Men are frustrated and women are frustrated. Why? Consider what women say about men:

- They are too task-oriented.
- They have only one thing on their minds.
- They are horrible listeners.
- They are too independent.
- They are emotionally shallow.
- They are always trying to "fix" problems.

Now consider what men say about women:

- They are overly relational.
- They want and give too many details.
- They want to "process" everything verbally.
- They are too emotional.
- They try to change and control us.
- They don't respect us enough.

Can you relate? You probably already know how easy it is to get into a relationship with a woman, but it's not so easy to make the relationship work well. It takes energy. It demands effort. It requires education. Funny how we know these things intuitively. Not so funny how we fail to apply them in our relationships with women.

None of us would ever embark on an important project, a significant career change, or a major athletic challenge without gathering all the tactical knowledge possible to ensure a good outcome. Yet when it comes to relationships with women, most of us fail to apply the simple principles that make us successful in other areas of life.

Want some great news? God says He's available to help, if we choose to accept it. But there's a catch: God's man must truly connect with God's purposes before he can truly connect with his wife (or potential bride). God uses our relationships with women to promote growth in our lives because it shows us where we come up short and drives us to Him for solutions. He knows the quality of that relationship will never surpass the depth of our character. And character is His specialty. If we want true intimacy and connection with a woman, we need to grow up and graduate from God's school of character. This is where we trust God will bring you through this study. We hope you'll experience many breakthroughs in your beliefs and character so that these changes will impact your relationship with a woman.

In the end, connecting with a woman can't only be about her if you are God's man. "What?" you say. That's right; it's not about her! Instead, it's about God's plan for your life. It's about following that plan faithfully and obediently. It's about seeing your relationship as an instrument for making you into the man God wants you to be. It's about pursuing the truth about yourself, recognizing when God (not your wife or girlfriend) is calling you to change, then making the change for Him (not for her). It's about getting in touch with the passion and love of Jesus Christ, allowing His acceptance and forgiveness of you to produce deeper appreciation and acceptance of her. It's about becoming like Jesus Christ, who was free to love, engage with, and serve others radically. He could do this because He lived for an audience of One. And this same Jesus lives in you.

Warning: The Enemy does not want you connecting with a woman in the ways outlined in this study. If fact, he will use every fear and every sour thought to dissuade you. Why? Because if he can isolate you from God's purposes for your relationship, he can destroy that relationship. Just know that by choosing to participate in this study, you have decided to pick a fight. You have decided to be proactive and say no to disconnection from God and the woman you love. Instead, you're saying yes to God's plan for connection and real intimacy.

Our goal in this study is to stimulate personal reflection and honest dialogue with God and with other husbands (or future husbands) about these matters. As you work through each session, look in the mirror at your own life and ask yourself some hard questions. Whether you are doing this study individually or in a group, realize that complete honesty with yourself, with God, and with others will produce the best results.

Our prayer is that you will be moved to embrace God's plan for connecting with the woman in your life. May you experience great blessing as you risk becoming God's man in the relationship and grow in your understanding of a woman's heart.

trust!

I Want the Right Motive

Key Verse

He who has My commandments and keeps them is the one who loves Me. (John 14:21, NASB)

Goals for Growth

- Expose wrong motives in my relationship with my wife.
- Adopt the right motives for pursuing change in our relationship.
- Experience a closer relationship with Christ.

Head Start

In *My Utmost for His Highest,* Oswald Chambers wrote, "If things are dark to me, then I may be sure there is something I will not do. Intellectual darkness comes through ignorance; spiritual darkness comes because of something I do not intend to obey."

His point? We deliberately ignore certain things because becoming informed would call for changing the way we live and think. When it comes to our relationship with our wife, instead of becoming a student of her needs, we choose to remain ignorant so we can continue the relational status quo. We cling to the surest, safest, most selfish lifestyle.

So how do we cross over from intentional ignorance to the pursuit of understanding a woman's heart? As Todd and I (Kenny) minister to men, we do see guys trying to connect and respond appropriately to their wife's needs. But the majority of guys seem to fail for one simple reason: their motives are messed up.

Consider some of the popular motives for what we might call "pseudotransformation" in a relationship:

- To win certain immediate favors (wink, wink).
- To end an argument and restore "order."
- To placate her in hopes that she'll return the favor.
- To get her to change.
- To gain control in the relationship.
- To extort a favor later on (triple wink).

All of these motives may seem right and good, even logical in the moment. But over the long haul, they result only in disappointment, resentment, and manipulation. They don't bring about lasting change in you or in the relationship. In the end, doing certain things to gain certain responses prevents us from deeply connecting with a woman.

And, of course, a woman is already suspicious of your motivations, especially when you miraculously morph prior to crawling into bed with her and then revert to your old style afterward. What makes the situation even worse is when she sees your resentment being directed at her because you feel as if she's forcing you to change.

Now think: What if your focus shifted from doing the right thing for her to being God's man? What pressure would this take off her and out of the relationship? How would that free you to pursue change in the way you relate to her? How would that free her to embrace the changes you make? Yes, it's good to want our wife's affections and approval. But connecting with her as God's man must be about winning *His* approval.

The foundation of true connection is trust, and trust thrives when two people feel safe with each other. A relationship becomes "unsafe" for a woman when she has to push or nag a man to change. The right motive for understanding what a woman wants is not to curry her favor, but to obey God's command to "live with [her] in an understanding way" (1 Peter 3:7, NASB). So whether you've been married for fifty years or five years—or are single and have been dating for five months—if you are God's man and are connected to a woman, class is always in session.

Connect with the Word

Read 1 Peter 3:7 (NASB).

1. What two commands speak to the husband in this text? Why do you think God instructs husbands to focus on these two areas?

2. What does the command for a husband to understand his wife imply about the way men typically approach relationships with women?

What does this command imply about the way God views women?

3. What do you think it means to "live with your wives in an understanding way"? What does it mean for you in terms of everyday living?

4. What does the command for a husband to honor his wife suggest about God's attitude toward women?

5. According to this verse, when should we apply these commands to our lives?

6. What consequence will we experience if we do not heed these commands?

7. What does this tell you about God's heart and His desire for your relationship with your wife?

Connect with the Group

Group Opener
Read the group opener aloud and discuss the questions that follow.
(Suggestion: As you begin your group discussion time in each of the following sessions, consider forming smaller groups of three to six men. This will allow more time for discussion and give everyone an opportunity to share their struggles.)

I [Fred] had trampled Brenda, crushing the opportunity for oneness in our marriage. I had stampeded her concerns, stepped on her feelings. Such trampling is sinning against your wife.

Yes, I said *sinning.* If you're thinking I'm off the wall and you're ready to put this book down, don't move so fast. Most of us Christian men sin against our wives regularly, but we're just too blind to see it. Odds are, you're a bit blind too. So why do I say *trampling* instead of *sinning?*

The word *sin* has lost its communication value in our culture partly because it's considered too judgmental. No one likes to be called a sinner. *That's for people who are really bad.*

More important, *sin* no longer has a consistent meaning among Christian men. While we can all agree that sin is bad, we have trouble agreeing upon what qualifies as sin. Most of us smugly believe that we never sin against our wives. Our Hit Parade of Sins comes from the Ten Commandments, and since we haven't stolen from or lied (oops) to our wives or cheated on them, we're in the clear, right?

Not really. Our definition of sin is far too narrow. Many of us go through life without understanding the full height, breadth, and depth of God's definition of sin. Instead of asking, "How holy can I be?" we prefer to ask, "How far can I go and still be called a Christian?"

And how far we go depends upon the benchmarks set by our peers rather than by God. Under such a scenario, we miss standing in the center of God's holy ground, preferring instead to roam the outer edges where we step outside the lines too often. And if we find a few Christian brothers out there with us, we simply move the boundaries out a bit farther.[1]

---

1. Stephen Arterburn and Fred Stoeker, *Every Man's Marriage* (Colorado Springs: WaterBrook, 2001), 23-24.

Discussion Questions

a. Do you think the writer's assessment is right: "Most of us Christian men sin against our wives regularly, but we are just too blind to see it"? Why or why not?

b. When have you trampled on your wife, crushing the opportunity for connection in your marriage?

c. Are you as consistent in assessing your own actions as you are in evaluating your wife's actions? Explain.

d. Why do you think husbands tend to cut themselves so much slack?

e. According to 1 Peter 3:7, why might we want to pursue a different way of relating to our wives?

f. Why are our wives often skeptical of our promises to change?

g. Think about the biblical motive you should have for connecting with your wife. What happens to the "control factor" in a marriage (the tendency of husband and wife to control each other) when a man obeys God?

h. How does having the right (Christ-centered) motivation for connecting make deeper intimacy between husband and wife possible?

i. What happens to a wife's nagging when God's man takes ownership of his need to change? How would that benefit the
relationship?

Standing Strong
What aspects of your connection with your wife would you like to be
different? Write down a few of your ideas.

What steps will you take to realize those goals?

Write a prayer expressing your desire to be God's man in your marriage. Let God know of your willingness (or unwillingness) to do what-
ever He asks or requires of you in the relationship. Invite God to
meet you right where you are.

acceptance

I Want to Be Loved with Christlike Love

Key Verse

God demonstrates his own love for us in this: While we were still sinners, Christ died for us. (Romans 5:8)

Goals for Growth

- Recognize that God loved me most when I deserved it least.
- Reflect this same love toward my wife.
- Recommit to assuring my wife verbally of my acceptance and appreciation.

Head Start

As I (Kenny) look back over the years, I'm amazed. It seems I've been more likely to extend much more patience, forgiveness, grace, and mercy to friends and strangers than to my own wife. This bugged Chrissy. Call it what you will; she called it hurtful. The weird thing is that many times I didn't even know I was hurting her—or couldn't seem to help myself.

Why do we hurt those we love the most? Clearly, friends and strangers have their faults, but their imperfections don't directly impact my life like the glaring shortcomings of those who live with me. I don't encounter other people's problems firsthand. Nor am I their guinea pig for creative experiments in family dysfunction. Consequently, this frees me to forgive other people's foibles and offer acceptance. After all, what do I have to lose? It's easy and it certainly doesn't require much character on my part.

With Chrissy, things are different. When her faults bubble to the surface, I'm right there. Her life intertwines with mine, and her problems are my problems. They get played out in our marriage and directly affect our ability to connect and communicate. Her weaknesses and the differences in our personalities that used to be cute before we got married now become sources of irritation. They can even begin festering into resentment.

And it's certainly not one-sided. This little river flows both ways! In fact, I would have to say that my sinful patterns offer the bigger challenge for the whole family.

Two questions for us, then, as we begin exploring a woman's desire for acceptance: First, how is God's man supposed to react to his wife's shortcomings? And second, how does God respond to my shortcomings and sin?

If God were to hold husbands to the same standard of acceptance that we impose upon our wives, wouldn't our relationship with Him instantly incinerate? We just don't deserve His acceptance. Yet He loves and accepts us even though we are guilty. Faultfinding is not His style. Being God's man—and a sinner—means it shouldn't be our style either.

Connect with the Word

Read John 8:2-11.

1. What were the teachers of the law and the Pharisees asking Jesus to do?

2. Was there a justification for exposing the woman's sin that made sense to her accusers? Jot down some of your insights about this.

3. To what extent was the woman's sin the real issue? What was the hidden agenda of the religious leaders?

4. Why do you think Jesus waited so long to answer?

5. What do you think of Jesus's answer to their question? What was His clear message to the accusers?

6. What do you think the woman expected to happen at crucial points of the situation?

7. Clearly, Jesus didn't ignore the woman's sin. What did He do instead?

8. What effect do you think Jesus's handling of the situation might have had on the woman in the days that followed?

Connect with the Group

Group Opener

Discuss the group-opener question and the discussion questions that follow.

How do you react when your wife's faults come out?

___ I magnify those faults.

___ I withhold love until she corrects her faults.

___ I love her in spite of her faults.

Explain your answer to the guys in your group.

Discussion Questions

a. Based upon your experience and/or observation, what impact does faultfinding have on a marital relationship? Give a specific example if you can.

b. What goes through a woman's mind when her husband criticizes her?

c. What fears does your wife have? What can you do to show her unconditional love and acceptance as she struggles with her fears?

d. How does negativity gain a foothold in a relationship? What can we do to avoid falling into that mentality?

e. Think about your family of origin and your upbringing. Recall how your parents related to each other and displayed affection—or how they failed in these areas. What impact does your family background have on your marriage relationship today?

f. What steps can you take to become more tender toward your wife?

Standing Strong

Ask your wife this week whether she feels loved and accepted by you. You might simply ask her, "What do I do that makes you feel loved and accepted or unloved and rejected?" Write some other possible questions below.

Spend a few minutes praying with your wife and express your desire to love and accept her based on God's love for you. (Plan to report to the group next week about what you did and said.)

connection

I Want You to Know Me Before You "Know" Me

Key Verse

My dear brothers, take note of this: Everyone should be quick to listen, slow to speak and slow to become angry. (James 1:19)

Goals for Growth

- Understand what listening communicates to a woman.
- Identify poor communication skills.
- Learn to listen to and be present with my wife.

Head Start

Our wives want to be known emotionally before they're "known" in the biblical sense. They long to be listened to on a deep level. This is a true language of love for a woman. In fact, not being listened to initiates a chain reaction in a woman's mind that goes like this: "He doesn't listen to me.... He doesn't care about me.... I will find some-one else to talk to who will listen to me.... I will experience caring from that person."

What makes matters worse is the way we men are hard-wired. Intimacy for us is spelled s-e-x. Intimacy for women is spelled t-a-l-k. Men tend to compartmentalize emotions. Women experience emo-tions as intricately connected to every other aspect of their lives.

Let's face it: Most men are horrible listeners, and it kills our con-nection with our wives. But in order to obey God and connect with our wives, we need face up to our weaknesses in communication and work on improving in those areas. It's an act of faith.

The reason many of us don't know how to communicate with our wives is because we've never seen healthy communication in action. Most men are stuck in emotional kindergarten and have to be taught. (I [Kenny] am one of them!) The good news is that just a little healthy communication goes a long way. For us men that means listening more and talking less. God has put our wives in our lives to help us develop a skill that we need to be good at as God's man.

But what does it mean to really listen? Marriage expert Gary Oliver defines it this way: "Listening means that when another per-son is speaking, you are not thinking about what you are going to say when the other person stops talking. Listening is choosing to be present."[2]

---

2. Gary Oliver, "Growing a Christ-Centered Marriage" (speech, Promise Keepers marriage seminar, John Brown University, Siloam Springs, AR, September 11, 2003).

The problem is that we're expert fakers. We can pretend to be present with a woman. We can maintain eye contact. We can smile. But our mind is focused on the TV sports story playing out in the background.

We are also pros at mental and verbal interruptions. We anticipate where the conversation is going, and we rush to beat people to their own conclusions. This might be a fun game we play, but it's disrespectful—and it's a sin.

Or maybe we start mentally rehearsing our responses and coming up with solutions before we've allowed our wife to finish her story. Or we just plain interrupt.

All of these modes of communication are unhealthy and disconnect us from our wives. We all know when somebody's not listening to us—and so do our wives. So what are you going to do about it?

Connect with the Word

Read James 1:19.

1. What commands do you find in this verse? What do these commands suggest about our tendencies in relationships?

2. Do you think learning to effectively listen to your wife is part of God's plan for you? Why or why not?

3. What do we communicate to others when we talk too much and listen too little?

4. What feelings are produced in others as a result of bad listening on our part?

5. How do you think God uses our listening in others' lives? How does it minister to them?

Read Proverbs 18:13-14.

6. What behavior is discouraged in verse 13?

7. When we answer before listening, what does this say about us?

8. What is one possible effect our lack of listening can have on our wives (verse 14)?

9. When we mentally or verbally answer before listening, what negative impact does this have on communication?

Connect with the Group

Group Opener
Read the group opener aloud and discuss the questions that follow.

Think back to those heady days of dating, when you couldn't drink in enough conversation from the young woman you knew you were going to marry. You loved listening to every thought, every wide-open hope, and all of her deepest dreams as you shared a bowl of nacho chips at the local eatery. Every opinion was a lovely thread in the tapestry she wove around your heart. But then things changed...

When the honeymoon is over and our differences follow us home, our wife's opinions feel more like binding cords threatening to choke our freedom and disrupt the peace. No guy would ever envision tuning out his lover before the wedding day, but in apartments, townhomes, condos, and starter homes across the fruited plain, countless men are snuffing out the voices of their wives seeking to express their views. What that does to oneness is not pretty, says Jerri:

> My husband usually gets mad because I'm not on the same
> wavelength that he is. This leads to a fight, and he'll say degrad-
> ing, belittling things to me. There's no compassion or consider-
> ation for my feelings. I've found that to be very hurtful.

To snuff out your wife's voice is to sin against her. It's also a sin against God because it blocks His purposes for your wife's voice in His kingdom.

Rene says she's an open person who finds it easy to share her feelings. Her husband, Paul, is a more private individual who shares few thoughts with other people, especially in Sunday school. Once when the couple was traveling home from church, the conversation went like this:

> "Why did you have to bring up our kids again in our couples'
> class?" he asked. "And while we're at it, why do you have to talk
> so much?"
> "I have experiences and insights that I just have to
> express," she replied.

Telling Rene to not exhale her thoughts would be like telling a whale not to spray water through its blowhole. Inwardly, each time

Paul told Rene to keep a lid on it, she felt as though she were an embarrassment to him. It wasn't as if she were giving away family secrets about the boys; they were a handful, that's all. *It must be something about me as a person that he doesn't like,* she thought. *Openness is who I am, and he was attracted to that quality when we were dating.*

The couple talked about it, but this impasse wasn't overcome in a day or even in several months. Over the years, however, after several people in their Sunday school class commented to Paul about how much Rene's sharing had helped them in their own lives, he slowly began to appreciate her transparency. He finally stopped telling Rene what she should or shouldn't say.

Most of your wife's gifts will be expressed through her thoughts and opinions. Her voice is the vehicle through which we husbands will be blessed, so stripping her of her voice by demanding that she clam up in public renders many of her God-given gifts useless. In addition, when you keep her from voicing opinions at home, the damage is infinitely greater.[3]

Discussion Questions

a. In general, would you say you make room for your wife's thoughts—or do you snuff them out? Explain.

---

3. Arterburn and Stoeker, *Every Man's Marriage,* 140-42.

b. In what ways can you relate to the author's description of the styles of communicating and listening before and after the wedding?

c. Why do men tend to invalidate the emotions of their wives by shutting conversation down or avoiding it altogether? What is our fear?

d. Why is it a sin against your wife to snuff out her voice and feelings?

e. Does becoming a good listener diminish your manhood? Why or why not?

f. Does your wife feel as if she has a significant voice in your life? (See Proverbs 31:11-12.) How do you know?

g. How might a significant increase in listening to your wife and engaging her opinion impact your relationship?

Standing Strong

List the obstacles that are preventing you from being a man who's "quick to listen and slow to speak." Then pray and ask God to help you understand and honor your wife by becoming a better listener.

Today, after things are shut down and the kids are in bed, ask your wife to tell you about her day. Give her your undivided attention for as long as she wants.

headship

I Want Spiritual Leadership

Key Verse

Now I want you to realize that the head of every man is Christ, and the head of the woman is man, and the head of Christ is God. (1 Corinthians 11:3)

Goals for Growth

- Take responsibility for building a strong personal spiritual life.
- Promote and support spiritual values and actions in my marriage and family.
- Encourage my wife's spiritual gifts, pursuits, and dreams.

Head Start

As a men's pastor, I (Kenny) wind up getting lots of feedback from wives. What keeps surfacing? Over and over, it's spiritual leadership.

Wives express fatigue and frustration. They do a job they know is not theirs, but they do it anyway. By default.

Women long to be led spiritually. I've never been approached by a woman who told me, "I sure wish my husband would notch it back a little on the spiritual stuff." That's because God has given husbands the responsibility for spiritual leadership. In order to achieve God's purposes, spiritual leadership calls for submission among equals much the same way the Son submitted to the Father to carry out the plan of salvation. (See Ephesians 5:21.)

Submission to God, mutual submission to each other, and a wife's willing submission to her husband are all means of serving God. It's done by choice, not by force. And it deepens connection instead of creating distance. When done in alignment with God's purposes, submission makes everything else in the marriage relationship richer and more meaningful.

As husbands, we need to ask ourselves two key questions: What are my wife's spiritual needs, and how do I meet them?

Early in my marriage to Chrissy, I had no clue about how to serve and lead out of sacrificial love. It was all about me and what I was doing; she was simply along for the ride. I had my spiritual life, and she had hers. We were independent rather than interdependent. We prayed together, but our prayers were superficial (saying grace over meals, for example). We weren't connected in the most important way of all: spiritually.

What a mistake! I needed to make a U-turn.

Through the encouragement of friends and some very painful circumstances, I was prompted to change from my independent style to hands-on involvement in family leadership. Basically, I had to get a spiritual spine. I had to demonstrate doing the right thing as God's man in front of my entire family.

Over time this new focus gave me the credibility in Chrissy's eyes to lead her in other ways. Specifically, it allowed me to speak into her life and provide direction. Today she sees that I deeply care about her and what's going on in her spirit and in our family. She trusts my judgment and counsel more than ever. But I didn't start earning her trust and cooperation with words alone. It started with quiet action.

Connect with the Word

Read 1 Corinthians 11:3.

1. According to this verse, to whom is the man responsible?

2. Why does God emphasize the man's submission to Him before He assigns the man a position of spiritual leadership in the marriage?

3. What confidence should this sequence give a woman with respect to her husband's leadership? Do you see this type of confidence in your own wife? Explain.

4. What happens when men don't follow God's leadership sequence?

5. What purpose did Jesus's submission to His Father serve while He was a man on earth? What did He model for us that we can apply to our marriages?

6. What is the role of the head for a physical body? How does this metaphor apply to spiritual headship in marriage?

Read Ephesians 5:21,25-33.

7. In your own words, describe the analogy between a spiritual relationship (Christ and the church) and a human relationship (husband and wife).

8. According to verse 25, how are spiritual love and leadership expressed?

9. What was the main reason Jesus "gave himself up" (verses 26-27)? How does Jesus's example apply to you and your responsibility in your marriage (verse 28)? What are you called to do?

Connect with the Group

Group Opener

Discuss the group-opener question and the discussion questions that follow.

Think back over your years of marriage. How has your own walk with God affected your ability to provide spiritual leadership for your wife and family?

Discussion Questions

a. To what extent does your wife trust your walk with Christ? How do you know? How has this affected her level of trust in your leadership in other aspects of your relationship?

b. Was your own father the head of your household? In what ways does his example in spiritual leadership affect you today— positively or negatively?

c. Does your wife see you as the spiritual leader in your marriage? Why or why not?

d. In what ways, if any, do you encourage your wife to grow spiritually?

e. Do you lead out of a heart of serving your wife? If so, give an example. If not, what is your motivation for leading?

f. What, if anything, is God calling you to consider doing differently so that you can better connect with your wife's need for spiritual leadership?

g. How can this group help you achieve a greater level of spiritual connection with your wife?

Standing Strong

Jot down one new way you can connect with your wife spiritually this week. Be specific. (For example: pray with her, serve her quietly, do a project she needs done, take over reading the Bible to the kids before bedtime.)

Reread Ephesians 5:25-33 and reflect on your responsibility as a husband. Pray for God's direction and His support of your efforts to meet your wife's need for spiritual leadership.

encouragement

I Want to Feel Special to You

Key Verses

May our Lord Jesus Christ himself and God our Father, who loved us and by his grace gave us eternal encouragement and good hope, encourage your hearts and strengthen you in every good deed and word. (2 Thessalonians 2:16-17)

Goals for Growth

- Recognize that prioritizing our relationship makes my wife feel secure.
- Learn what encourages a woman.
- Initiate and integrate behaviors that encourage her.

Head Start

You can see it at the earliest ages. Little girls want to feel special. I (Kenny) see it in my five-year-old daughter Jenna. I see it in her eyes when I sing her "The Good Morning Song." Her whole counte-nance and body language morph when I greet her with a "Hello, my sugarplum diamond!" Her face turns sheepishly red when I ask if I can hold her hand…and then I kiss it. She grins from ear to ear when I sign "I love you" from across the room with a wink. She's on top of the world when she's resting in my arms. My little girl is encouraged by my words, by my presence, by my time, and by my understanding her need to feel like the apple of my eye.

Fast-forward twenty, thirty, even forty years. Will the "big girl" still thrive on the man in her life making her his special focus? Will she blush when his extra effort makes her feel as if she's the only one in the room? Will her need—her dream—of feeling wanted, valued, and appreciated have died? You know the answer to that question: Absolutely not!

Sadly, the ability of men to encourage women seems to be a lost art these days. Men have abandoned the princess inside their wives and instead have embraced them as mere co-workers. As a result, women's dreams have died and their loving hearts toward their hus-bands have withered. Women have become so accustomed to the routine, the roles, and the repetition in their marriage that they feel about as special as the furniture.

The myth we men embrace is that after the "conquest" we can "coast" on the encouragement front. That lie shows a complete disregard for how God has created a woman, and it kills intimacy in the relationship. When a man stops encouraging his wife and making her feel special, she feels deceived and ripped off. Over time the painful truth—that it was all a game, and she was simply a prize—begins to sink in. The result: A man loses his credibility and the respect that goes with it. A woman cannot be fully intimate with a man she does not respect and even resents.

Many of us grew up in families that were devoid of encouragement, so it's hard for us to extend it to others. But regardless of our backgrounds, we have received in Jesus Christ the deep and healing encouragement we need to break this destructive pattern. When we get in touch with how much God loves to encourage us, we are able to give away the same encouragement to others daily. We can encourage our wives through our understanding, time, and verbal appreciation.

So…has the princess inside your wife died? What are you going to do to bring her back to life?

Connect with the Word

Read Psalm 139:1-6.

1. What does God know about David (verses 1-4)? How is David's connection with God unique and different from his relationships with others?

2. What impact does it have on David to know that God understands what makes him tick (verse 6)?

3. Does it encourage you to know that God understands you and your needs? Explain.

4. How aware are you of God's knowing and loving presence with you throughout the day? What would help increase your awareness?

Read Deuteronomy 33:12.

5. What word describes God's people in this verse?

6. What attitudes and actions should being the "beloved of the LORD" produce in His people?

7. What does placing His people "between his shoulders" say about God?

8. In what ways does God's presence and closeness encourage you?

Read Proverbs 16:24.

9. How do words of encouragement differ from other kinds of words?

10. What are some of the positive outcomes of verbal encouragement?

11. When have you been most blessed by someone's encouraging words? (*Suggestion:* Replay the event in your mind and bask in it for a few prayerful moments.)

Connect with the Group

Group Opener
Read the group opener aloud and discuss the questions that follow.

Go into any restaurant and watch the older couples. Most take a small corner table, order off the menu, and barely speak a word to each other during the entire meal. Their eyes rarely meet. As they shuffle past on their way out the door, look at the woman's eyes. It's truly harrowing. She's just playing out the string. Was this God's dream for her in marriage? For us? In premarriage class, every female eye is bright with hope and anticipation. The trampling of marriage brings death to those eyes.

Your wife didn't expect you to trample her. You seemed kind and godly before marriage. She never dreamed you would treat her like this. In premarriage class, we ask women, "What impresses you most about your fiancé?" Their answers are beautiful:

Denise: "What impresses me the most is his kindness and honesty."

Karen: "He's so attentive and respectful."

Penny: "I'm most impressed with his patience."

Marsha: "He's a very compassionate guy."

Amy: "He's so caring and sensitive toward me."

Jodie: "He's just such an encourager."

Ruth: "He shows such patience in our impasses."

Diane: "He wants to do anything and everything to be a better husband."

Ten years from now, will these same women say that they'd been snowed by their husbands?

What impressed your wife the most about you before you got married? Do you still impress her in this way? Are you still an encourager? Do you still have patience in the impasses? Are you attentive and respectful enough to submit to oneness?

Kindness, patience, respect, honesty, and compassion are necessary for male submission. Perhaps your wife once saw these things in you. Were they a mirage? Your soul once seemed a cool pool in her dry and thirsty land, and she dived headlong into marriage in total trust. Did she find a companionship or a mouthful of sand?[4]

Discussion Questions

a. Think about your marriage. Has your wife found a companion or a "mouthful of sand"? Explain.

---

4. Arterburn and Stoeker, *Every Man's Marriage,* 59-60.

b. What behaviors demonstrate a desire to understand your wife? What actions demonstrate the opposite?

c. Would your wife say she is a priority in your life? Why or why not? What evidence can she point to?

d. What time each day have you specifically set aside just to be with your wife? What is the purpose for your time together? (For example: to discuss the kids, to debrief on your days, to enjoy each other's company, etc.)

e. Does your wife ever hear you brag about her? When was the last time you praised her in front of others?

f. In general, do you build up your wife more than you tear her down? What can you do to improve in this area?

Standing Strong

Think about the three ways women feel encouraged. Which is your weakest area?

____ understanding my wife

____ spending time with her

____ offering her verbal encouragement

Pray and ask God for wisdom to know how to encourage your wife in this area. Then write down three practical steps you can take to improve in this area.

Example: offering verbal encouragement

1. Praise her three times a day.

2. Brag about her in front of the kids.

3. Pray with her before going to sleep—and thank God for her.

Trust God to help you during the coming week to encourage your wife in these ways.

friendship

I Want "Us"

Key Verse

The LORD God said, "It is not good for the man to be alone. I will make a helper suitable for him." (Genesis 2:18)

Goals for Growth

- Understand the importance of togetherness to a woman.
- Commit to God's purpose of oneness with my wife.
- Build new connections with my wife to make her a full partner and a prized friend.

Head Start

Listen to how Glenn talks on the phone with Mitch, his mountain biking buddy:

"Hey, Mitch. Glenn. Bro, what's happening?"

"Right now, all I'm thinking about is us scoring a hall pass from the wives this Saturday and hitting Santa Ana Canyon Trail for a burner ride."

"Oh, great idea. I think our wives will let us off the reservation if we can get on the trail at the crack of dawn," Glenn says.

"Dawn patrol? Hmmm. Yeah, we gotta do it. I need to get a ride in. Let's work on that. Did you eat lunch yet?"

"No, I am starving. Does a Mione's sausage sandwich sound good to you?"

"Sure does. Let's beat the rush. Will 11:45 work for you?"

"I'll be there, and I'll bring that article I found about your bike."

"Cool, see ya there in fifteen. Later."[5]

I (Kenny) wrote about Mitch and Glenn's friendship to illustrate how "into" each other they are. It's easy to have this kind of manly connection with another guy, especially when toys and hobbies are involved.

Close friendships between guys are rare and special. Lots of love and respect flow back and forth. You're always looking for ways to encourage a prized friend. You ask him about his future and his life path. You are into this relationship and monitor how it's going. You are protective in a healthy way and watch out for your friend's best interests.

Because you know your friend so well, you're able to bring out the best in him—and he brings out the best in you. You love him

5. Stephen Arterburn and Kenny Luck, *Every Man, God's Man* (Colorado Springs: WaterBrook, 2003), 177-78.

enough to tell him the truth, yet you never tear him down. You are a safe place for him to go, and he is your safe harbor.

Sadly, many of the men we counsel are emotionally closer to and more authentic with their guy friends than they are with their own wives. Let's be clear: A man needs his guy friends, but God's plan is for his wife to be his number-one human confidante and a guiding influence in his life. A man dishonors his wife by not recognizing her desire to be his confidante and a trusted source of counsel. More important, he disobeys God when he turns to friends before turning to his wife on the big issues that affect both of them.

Is a paradigm shift in order?

Connect with the Word

Read Genesis 2:18-25.

1. In verse 18, what word describes the woman's purpose in being a counterpart to the man? What does this suggest about God's assessment of Adam?

2. According to verse 23, how does Adam view God's gift to him of Eve? What is Adam's commitment?

Rewrite this verse in your own words.

3. What characterizes the connection between the man and the woman (verse 24)?

4. In what ways are a man and woman to experience togetherness? (*Hint:* Base your response on your own experience as well as Scripture.)

5. How does the absence of shame and guilt help Adam and Eve's relationship (verse 25)?

6. Do you think it is important for a man to be fully known by his wife? Why or why not? How well does your wife know you? What's the basis for your answer?

Read Proverbs 31:10-12.

7. What value is ascribed to the wife in this passage (verse 10)?

8. According to verse 11, what benefits does the husband of such a wife enjoy?

9. What are the wife's motives with respect to her husband's welfare (verse 12)?

10. In your own words, describe the partnership illustrated in this passage.

Connect with the Group

Group Opener
Discuss the group-opener question and the discussion questions that follow.

Would your wife consider herself your confidante? Why or why not? (Give specific examples to support your response.)

Discussion Questions

a. What stands out to you as most important in this session on spiritual friendship with a woman?

b. Would you describe your style of connection with your wife as independent or interdependent? Why?

c. To what extent do you invite your wife into your private world? Do you allow her to point out shortcomings she sees in your life? How do you respond when she does?

d. Do you practice spiritual accountability with your wife? Why or why not? What would spiritual accountability to your wife look like in practical terms?

e. How often do you ask for your wife's input when you make decisions? If you never ask for her input, why don't you?

What can the group do to hold you accountable in this area?

f. What activities do you and your wife do together?

g. Do you know what your wife's dreams are? When was the last
    time you asked her?

Standing Strong

Review the following list[6] and select one or two areas of togetherness
you can work on to cultivate your friendship with your wife.

___ emotional togetherness: being tuned in to each other's needs

___ intellectual togetherness: sharing thoughts, ideas, opinions, and
     beliefs

___ aesthetic togetherness: enjoying the beauty and artistry of life

___ recreational togetherness: having fun and excitement as a couple

___ work togetherness: doing common, everyday tasks as a team

___ crisis togetherness: leaning on each other when times are hard

___ sexual togetherness: bonding through physical closeness

___ spiritual togetherness: drawing closer to God and encouraging
     each other in the faith

What practical actions will you take to cultivate friendship with your
wife in the area(s) you identified?

---

6. Created by Steve Stephens, PhD.

thoughtfulness

I Want to Be Remembered by You

Key Verse

"I know the plans I have for you," declares the LORD, "plans to prosper you and not to harm you, plans to give you hope and a future." (Jeremiah 29:11)

Goals for Growth

- Learn to listen more thoughtfully to my wife.
- Actively direct my thoughts toward her.
- Seek unplanned opportunities to bless her.

Head Start

I (Kenny) will never forget the first time I blew Chrissy's mind. We had just started dating and were getting to know each other on a deeper level after being "friends" at UCLA for about four months. Let's just say that the infatuation factor was high and the need to impress ran deep. During this phase of our lives, connecting over coffee was an affordable way to enjoy each other's company.

During one of our "coffee talks," Chrissy told me about a "cute" jacket she had found at a boutique in Westwood. Unfortunately, the price was way too high, so she left the jacket on the rack.

As soon as she started describing the jacket, a loud bell went off inside my head, and I started spinning my web. I thought, *Be cool— interested but disinterested in this little jacket.* So I deliberately sipped my coffee, and then I said, "Oh, really? You liked it, huh? What color was it?" Then I subtly managed to slip in, "So they had your size and everything?"

I needed more details. "Was it, like, denim?" You see, I was writing down the pertinent info on a binder below table level. Eventually, though, we both had to get to class.

"Bummer that jacket was so expensive," I said, and that was that.

Or was it? Within two hours I was in that boutique plunking down sixty bucks of hard-earned money to win the day—and the heart of my green-eyed beauty. (Don't throw up.)

While Chrissy was in class, I went to her apartment, and one of her roommates let me put the jacket on Chrissy's bed. When she got back from class, the "Hallelujah Chorus" broke out in that little apartment. At least for that day, Spider-Man got the girl.

What message did my actions send to Chrissy? *He was thinking of me! He was really listening. He took mental notes. He planned creatively. He acted imaginatively. He invested time and treasure in me. He surprised me with a special treat. He was looking for a way to encourage me. He sacrificed his entire afternoon!*

Most men think, *Well, that was then. This is now.* But the reality is this: If that's how she thought and felt and loved it then, that's how she thinks and feels today. And that's how I still need to act today.

You may be asking, So what does this have to do with being God's man? The answer: God does all those things with us. We are on His mind. He knows our heart's desires and makes creative plans to fulfill them in His time. He surprises us with blessings. He seeks specific ways to encourage us. He sacrificed His Son for the joy of connecting with us. He lives in you and wants to bless your wife through you.

God loves thoughtfulness because it reflects His character. Are you reflecting Him today in your actions toward your wife?

Connect with the Word

Read 1 Samuel 1:1-20.

1. What was Hannah's deeply felt need? Why was this so important to her? What was the long-term impact of not receiving
   what she longed for? What toll did it take?

2. According to verse 11, what four things did Hannah ask of God? What was His response (verse 19)?

3. Read 1 Samuel 2:1. What effect did God's remembrance of Hannah have on her relationship with Him?

Read Luke 1:46-49.

4. In your own words, describe Mary's thoughts and feelings.

5. What did God do (in Mary's words) to prompt this response?

6. What does Mary's reaction to God's "mindfulness" of her tell us about the heart of a woman?

7. What instrument do you think God wants to use to bless and encourage your wife? In what specific ways could you bless and encourage her?

8. How can your being thoughtful improve your wife's relationship with God?

Connect with the Group

Group Opener

Discuss the group-opener question and the discussion questions that follow.

What obstacles keep you from "remembering" your wife and showing her thoughtfulness and consideration?

Discussion Questions

a. List some practical ways you can show your wife consideration and thoughtfulness. (*Hint:* What tangibles and intangibles are important to her? What does she value the most?)

b. How can you discover what is most important to your wife?

c. What is your wife's "love language"? In other words, what helps her feel loved by you? (For example: your acts of service, gifts, having time to shop alone, getting help with household chores, etc.)

d. How do you think your wife would respond to more spontaneous acts of thoughtfulness on your part? What opportunities will you have today to take a step in this direction?

e. What sacrifices or changes will you need to make in order to be more thoughtful of your wife?

f. What will you gain in the long term from investing in your marriage in this way?

g. How will being more thoughtful of your wife make you a better "God's man"?

Standing Strong

Write down one way you can show thoughtfulness toward your wife this week. Share with the group what you are going to do.

Pray as a group for the action step each of you will be taking. Ask God to use you to encourage your wife. Be prepared to share at your next meeting what you did, how your wife responded, and how God used this exercise in your life.

compassion

I Want a Strong Man with a Soft Heart

Key Verse

Even in darkness light dawns for the upright, for the gracious and compassionate and righteous man. (Psalm 112:4)

Goals for Growth

- Recognize that compassion is a core character quality of God.
- Develop this quality in my own character.
- Practice compassion toward my wife and others.

Head Start

Most men aren't trained to be compassionate. Instead, we're taught as little boys to push down or push away feelings of empathy. We're told to "be a man." All dads, for the most part, want their boys to develop a thick skin—the mental and emotional toughness required to stand up and stand out.

Many of us have learned to be boot-camp boys. We are stoic and show limited emotion. Being insensitive helps us in some environments (such as in sports and business), but it is disastrous for our relationships, especially with women. Our inability to express our emotions not only hurts us in our relationships with women but in our ability to connect with the needs of those around us. It fuels the perception that we are insensitive even though this is usually not the case. We just have a tough time identifying with the feelings of others or even expressing our own feelings. We are untrained in these areas.

I (Kenny) am terrible at this business of feelings. I know I'm bad at identifying emotions. I don't validate emotional reasoning. I don't trust feelings, and I perceive those who do as weak in some way. I was trained to think that being emotional is weak and unmanly. This like-an-oak style is okay in many settings, but it simply doesn't play with most women. And over time it will damage or destroy our connection with them. More important, this style is inconsistent with a being a serious follower of Jesus Christ.

Jesus displayed a full range of emotion. The Bible tells us that He was often moved with compassion by the needs and losses of those around Him. In some cases, He was even moved to tears. Jesus had a spine for doing what was right, yet He also had a heart for people. This Spirit of the same Jesus lives in God's man and is seeking expression, beginning with our relationship with our wives.

A strong man with a soft heart—that's Jesus. Let's open up to His way in this area.

Connect with the Word

Read Luke 7:11-17.

1. Why was the widow's situation so serious for a woman of that day?

2. How did Jesus respond to the woman (verse 13)? What emotional reaction did Jesus experience before He expressed compassion verbally to the woman?

3. What do you think was going through the woman's mind when Jesus entered the situation? after He left?

4. Have you, like the widow, experienced God's compassion? If so, how?

Read Luke 15:11-24.

5. What did the younger son have to experience before he came to his senses?

6. What do you think was going through his mind as he started home (verse 20)?

7. What did Jesus want His listeners to know about His Father in this parable?

8. Look at verse 20 again. What emotional and physical process was involved in the father's response to his son?

9. What enabled the father to express so much energy and compassion toward his son?

10. Do you think the father's overwhelmingly compassionate response matched the reaction the son had been expecting? Why or why not?

Connect with the Group

Group Opener
Discuss the group-opener question and the discussion questions that follow.

To what extent was your father a compassionate man? In what ways do you think his ability—or inability—to show compassion impacts you today?

Discussion Questions
a. Based on the Bible passages you've studied, what does it mean to be compassionate?

b. How do you usually respond to people who are experiencing great loss or remorse?

c. How do you respond when your wife needs emotional support?

d. Based on the parable of the prodigal son, what experience should drive God's man toward a lifestyle of compassion and caring?

e. Finish the following sentence, using as many different descriptions as possible:

God's compassion is...

f. How does your wife expect you to react when she shares a struggle she's experiencing? What does this tell you? (*Think:* Do I feel her pain and enter into it? Or do I avoid it and let her work things out?)

g. What practical first steps can a man take to develop a soft heart without sacrificing a strong personality?

h. Let your imagination go for a moment: What impact would developing Christlike compassion have on your marriage?

Standing Strong
List some ways you could begin reaching out compassionately to those whom God has put in your life. Start with your wife and family, then include others.

Write a short prayer thanking God for His mercy and compassion toward you. Ask Him to give you eyes to see and the courage to help those who need to experience His compassion through you.

small-group resources

What if men aren't doing the Connect with the Word section before our small-group session?

Don't be discouraged. You set the pace. If you are doing the study and regularly referring to it in conversations with your men throughout the week, they will pick up on its importance. Here are some suggestions to motivate the men in your group to do their home Bible study:

- Send out a midweek e-mail in which you share your answer to one of the study questions. This shows them that you are personally committed to and involved in the study.
- Ask the guys to hit "respond to all" on their e-mail program and share one insight from that week's Bible study with the entire group. Encourage them to send it out before the next small-group session.
- Every time you meet, ask each man in the group to share one insight from his home study.

What if men are not showing up for small group?

This might mean they are losing a sin battle and don't want to admit it to the group. Or they might be consumed with other priorities. Or maybe they don't think they're getting anything out of the group. Here are some suggestions for getting the guys back each week:

- Affirm them when they show up, and tell them how much it means to you that they make small group a priority.

- From time to time, ask them to share one reason small group is important to them.
- Regularly call or send out an e-mail the day before you meet to remind them you're looking forward to seeing them.
- Check in with any guy who has missed more than one session and find out what's going on in his life.
- Get some feedback from the men. You may need to adjust your style. Listen and learn.

What if group discussion is not happening?

You are a discussion facilitator. You have to keep guys involved in the discussion or you'll lose them. You can engage a man who isn't sharing by saying, "Chuck, you've been quiet. What do you think about this question or discussion?" You should also be prepared to share your own personal stories that are related to the discussion questions. You'll set the example by the kind of sharing you do.

What if one man is dominating the group time?

You have to deal with it. If you don't, men will stop showing up. No one wants to hear from just one guy all the time. It will quickly kill morale. Meet with the guy in person and privately. Firmly but gently suggest that he allow others more time to talk. Be positive and encouraging, but truthful. You might say, "Bob, I notice how enthusiastic you are about the group and how you're always prepared to share your thoughts with the group. But there are some pretty quiet guys in the group too. Have you noticed? Would you be willing to help me get them involved in speaking up?"

How do I get the guys in my group more involved?

Give them something to do. Ask one guy to bring a snack. Invite another to lead the prayer time (ask in advance). Have a guy sub for you one week as the leader. (Meet with him beforehand to walk through the group program and the time allotments for each segment.) Encourage another guy to lead a subgroup.

What if guys are not being vulnerable during the Standing Strong or prayer times?

You model openness. You set the pace. Honesty breeds honesty. Vulnerability breeds vulnerability. Are you being vulnerable and honest about your own problems and struggles? (This doesn't mean that you have to spill your guts each week or reveal every secret of your life.) Remember, men want an honest, on-their-level leader who strives to walk with God. (Also, as the leader, you need an accountability partner, perhaps another group leader.)

What will we do at the first session?

We encourage you to open by discussing the **Small-Group Covenant** we've included in this resource section. Ask the men to commit to the study, and then discuss how long it will take your group to complete each session. (We suggest 75-90 minute sessions.) Men find it harder to come up with excuses for missing a group session if they have made a covenant to the other men right at the start.

Begin to identify ways certain men can play a more active role in small group. Give away responsibility. You won't feel as burdened, and your men will grow from the experience. Keep in mind that this process can take a few weeks. Challenge men to fulfill one of the group roles identified later in this resource section. If no one steps forward to fill a role, say to one of the men, "George, I've noticed that you are comfortable praying in a group. Would you lead us each week during that time?"

How can we keep the group connected after we finish a study?
Begin talking about starting another Bible study before you finish this eight-week study. (There are several other studies to choose from in the Every Man Bible study series.) Consider having a social time at the conclusion of the study, and encourage the men to invite a friend. This will help create momentum and encourage growth as you launch into another study with your group. There are probably many men in your church or neighborhood who aren't in small groups but would like to be. Be the kind of group that includes others.

As your group grows, consider choosing an apprentice leader who can take half the group into another room for the **Connect with the Group** time. That subgroup can stay together for prayer, or you can reconvene as a large group during that time. You could also meet for discussion as a large group and then break into subgroups for **Standing Strong** and **prayer.**

If your group doubles in size, it might be a perfect opportunity to release your apprentice leader with half the group to start another group. Allow men to pray about this and make a decision as a group. Typically, the relational complexities that come into play when a small group births a new group work themselves out. Allow guys to choose which group they'd like to be a part of. If guys are slow in choosing one group or another, ask them individually to select one of the groups. Take the lead in making this happen.

Look for opportunities for your group to serve in the church or community. Consider a local outreach project or a short-term missions trip. There are literally hundreds of practical ways you can serve the Lord in outreach. Check with your church leaders to learn the needs in your congregation or community. Create some interest by sending out scouts who will return with a report for the group. Serving keeps men from becoming self-focused and ingrown. When you serve as a group, you will grow as a group.

using this study in a large-group format

Many church leaders are looking for biblically based curriculum that can be used in a large-group setting, such as a Sunday-school class, or for small groups within an existing larger men's group. Each of the Every Man Bible studies can be adapted for this purpose. In addition, this curriculum can become a catalyst for churches wishing to launch men's small groups or to build a men's ministry.

Getting Started

Begin by getting the word out to men in your church, inviting them to join you for a men's study based on one of the topics in the Every Man Bible study series. You can place a notice in your church bulletin, have the pastor announce it from the pulpit, or pursue some other means of attracting interest.

Orientation Week

Arrange your room with round tables and chairs. Put approximately six chairs at each table.

Start your session in prayer and introduce your topic with a short but motivational message from any of the scriptures used in the Bible study. Hand out the curriculum and challenge the men to do their homework before each session. During this first session give the men some discussion questions based upon an overview of the material and have them talk things through within their small group around the table.

Just before you wrap things up, have each group select a table host or leader. You can do this by having everyone point at once to the person at their table they feel would best facilitate discussion for future meetings.

Ask those newly elected table leaders to stay after for a few minutes, and offer them an opportunity to be further trained as small-group leaders as they lead discussions throughout the course of the study.

Subsequent Weeks

Begin in prayer. Then give a short message (15-25 minutes) based upon the scripture used for that lesson. Pull out the most motivating topics or points, and strive to make the discussion relevant to the everyday life and world of a typical man. Then leave time for each table to work through the discussion questions listed in the curriculum. Be sure the discussion facilitators at each table close in prayer.

At the end of the eight sessions, you might want to challenge each "table group" to become a small group, inviting them to meet regularly with their new small-group leader and continue building the relationships they've begun.

prayer request record

Date:

Name:

Prayer Request:

Praise:

Date:

Name:

Prayer Request:

Praise:

Date:

Name:

Prayer Request:

Praise:

Date:

Name:

Prayer Request:

Praise:

Date:

Name:

Prayer Request:

Praise:

defining group roles

Group Leader: Leads the lesson and facilitates group discussion.

Apprentice Leader: Assists the leader as needed, which may include leading the lesson.

Refreshment Coordinator: Maintains a list of who will provide refreshments. Calls group members on the list to remind them to bring what they signed up for.

Prayer Warrior: Serves as the contact person for prayer between sessions. Establishes a list of those willing to pray for needs that arise. Maintains the prayer-chain list and activates the chain as needed by calling the first person on the list.

Social Chairman: Plans any desired social events during group sessions or at another scheduled time. Gathers members for planning committees as needed.

small-group roster

Name:
Address:
Phone: E-mail:

Name:
Address:
Phone: E-mail:

Name:
Address:
Phone: E-mail:

Name:
Address:
Phone: E-mail:

Name:
Address:
Phone: E-mail:

Name:
Address:
Phone: E-mail:

spiritual checkup

Your answers to the statements below will help you determine which areas you need to work on in order to grow spiritually. Mark the appropriate letter to the left of each statement. Then make a plan to take one step toward further growth in each area. Don't forget to pray for the Lord's wisdom before you begin. Be honest. Don't be overly critical or rationalize your weaknesses.

Y = Yes
S = Somewhat or Sometimes
N = No

My Spiritual Connection with Other Believers

____ I am developing relationships with Christian friends.
____ I have joined a small group.
____ I am dealing with conflict in a biblical manner.
____ I have become more loving and forgiving than I was a year ago.
____ I am a loving and devoted husband and father.

My Spiritual Growth

____ I have committed to daily Bible reading and prayer.
____ I am journaling on a regular basis, recording my spiritual growth.

____ I am growing spiritually by studying the Bible with others.

____ I am honoring God in my finances and personal giving.

____ I am filled with joy and gratitude for my life, even during trials.

____ I respond to challenges with peace and faith instead of anxiety and anger.

____ I avoid addictive behaviors (excessive drinking, overeating, watching too much TV, etc.).

Serving Christ and Others

____ I am in the process of discovering my spiritual gifts and talents.

____ I am involved in ministry in my church.

____ I have taken on a role or responsibility in my small group.

____ I am committed to helping someone else grow in his spiritual walk.

Sharing Christ with Others

____ I care about and am praying for those around me who are unbelievers.

____ I share my experience of coming to know Christ with others.

____ I invite others to join me in this group or for weekend worship services.

____ I am praying for others to come to Christ and am seeing this happen.

____ I do what I can to show kindness to people who don't know Christ.

Surrendering My Life for Growth

___ I attend church services weekly.

___ I pray for others to know Christ, and I seek to fulfill the Great Commission.

___ I regularly worship God through prayer, praise, and music, both at church and at home.

___ I care for my body through exercise, nutrition, and rest.

___ I am concerned about using my energy to serve God's purposes instead of my own.

My Identity in the Lord

___ I see myself as a beloved son of God, one whom God loves regardless of my sin.

___ I can come to God in all of my humanity and know that He accepts me completely. When I fail, I willingly run to God for forgiveness.

___ I experience Jesus as an encouraging Friend and Lord each moment of the day.

___ I have an abiding sense that God is on my side. I am aware of His gracious presence with me throughout the day.

___ During moments of beauty, grace, and human connection, I lift up praise and thanks to God.

___ I believe that using my talents to their fullest pleases the Lord.

___ I experience God's love for me in powerful ways.

small-group covenant

As a committed group member, I agree to the following:*

- **Regular Attendance.** I will attend group sessions on time and let everyone know in advance if I can't make it.
- **Group Safety.** I will help create a safe, encouraging environment where men can share their thoughts and feelings without fear of embarrassment or rejection. I will not judge other guys or attempt to fix their problems.
- **Confidentiality.** I will always keep to myself everything that is shared in the group.
- **Acceptance.** I will respect different opinions or beliefs and let Scripture be the teacher.
- **Accountability.** I will make myself accountable to the other group members for the personal goals I share.
- **Friendliness.** I will look for those around me who might join the group and explore their faith with other men.
- **Ownership.** I will prayerfully consider taking on a specific role within the group as the opportunity arises.
- **Spiritual Growth.** I will commit to establishing a daily quiet time with God, which includes doing the homework for this study. I will share with the group the progress I make and the struggles I experience as I seek to grow spiritually.

Signed: _____ Date: _____

---

* *Permission is given to photocopy and distribute this form to each man in your group. Review this covenant quarterly or as needed.*

about the authors

STEPHEN ARTERBURN is coauthor of the best-selling Every Man series. He is also founder and chairman of New Life Clinics, host of the daily *New Life Live!* national radio program, and creator of the Women of Faith conferences. A nationally known speaker and licensed minister, Stephen has authored more than forty books. He lives with his family in Laguna Beach, California.

KENNY LUCK is president and founder of Every Man Ministries, coauthor of *Every Man, God's Man* and its companion workbook, and coauthor of the Every Man Bible studies. He is the area leader for men's ministry and teaches a men's interactive Bible study at Saddleback Church in Lake Forest, California. He and his wife, Chrissy, have three children and reside in Trabuco Canyon, California.

TODD WENDORFF is a graduate of University of California, Berkeley, and holds a ThM from Talbot School of Theology. He serves as a teaching pastor at King's Harbor Church in Redondo Beach and is an adjunct professor at Biola University. He is an author of the Doing Life Together Bible study series. Todd and his wife, Denise, live with their three children in Rolling Hills Estates, California.

start a bible study
and connect with others
who want to be God's man.

Every Man Bible Studies are designed to help you discover, own, and build on convictions grounded in God's word. Available now in bookstores.